Dad

Share Your Life With Me

Created by Kathleen Lashier

Copyright © 2012 Linkages

To contact the author:

Linkages Memory Journals • P.O. Box 8282 • Des Moines, IA 50301
888-815-9063
www.mymemoryjournals.com

Printed in the U.S.A.
by G&R Publishing Co.

ISBN-13: 978-1-56383-416-5
ISBN-10: 1-56383-416-2

Distributed by:

CQ Products

507 Industrial Street • Waverly, IA 50677
800-887-4445 • Fax 800-886-7496

*What was your day
and date of birth?* ....

....

....

....

....

....

....

....

January 1

*Where were you born?
Be specific.* ....

....

....

....

....

....

....

....

January 2

Do you know any other circumstances of your birth (who was present, who delivered, etc.)?

January 3

If you have a childhood picture for me, put it in this space.

January 4

Name your brothers and sisters and their years of birth.

January 5

What was your
mother's full name?

January 6

What were your
mother's date/place and
circumstances of birth?

January 7

*What was your father's
full name?*

_____

_____

_____

_____

_____

_____

_____

*What was your father's
date/place and
circumstances of birth?*

_____

_____

_____

_____

_____

_____

_____

Name all the street addresses you can recall and/or all the communities you've lived in and years there.

January 10

January 11

What did your father do for a living?

January 12

*Did your mother work
outside the home?*

_____

_____

_____

_____

_____

_____

_____

_____

January 13

*Tell a nickname your
family gave you and
how you got it.*

_____

_____

_____

_____

_____

_____

_____

_____

January 14

*Tell of any other nicknames
in your family.*

_____
_____
_____
_____
_____
_____
_____
_____
_____

January 15

*Tell a fond memory
of your Grandpa.*

_____
_____
_____
_____
_____
_____
_____
_____
_____

January 16

*Tell a fond memory
of your Grandma.*

January 17

Tell about a favorite Aunt.

January 18

Tell about a favorite Uncle.

January 19

Relate an experience or memory of a cousin.

January 20

Did any relatives ever live with you? If not, then relate another memory of cousins, aunts or uncles.

January 21

*When it was time for
discipline, which parent
corrected you and how?*

January 22

*Tell about the naughtiest thing
you ever did. If you got caught,
describe the consequences.*

January 23

Who was the President
when you were born?

At what age did you first vote
and for whom did you cast
your first Presidential vote?

Did you ever see a President
or Vice-President in person?

Which of the Presidents in your
lifetime has been your favorite and why?

*Did you ever have an
imaginary friend?*

*What did you and your
brothers or sisters fight
about the most?*

*Tell about an experience or
event that drew you together.*

January 29

*Tell about the worst winter storm
that you can remember as a child.*

January 30

*What did you use to go sledding
down a hill in the snow?*

January 31

*What extras did you use for your snowman's
face, buttons, arms, hat, etc?*

February 1

*Do you have any ice skating
memories to share?*

February 2

*Share a memory about a weather-
related school cancellation.*

February 3

Do you have any knowledge of the origins of your family name?

How did you first smash a finger?

February 4

February 5

Who was the most famous
person you ever met as a child?

February 6

Tell about someone who had
a big influence on your life.

February 7

*Tell about another
influential person in your life.*

Tell about a big lie you told.

*What was your favorite
meal as a child?*

Who was your first
girlfriend?

Tell about the Valentine
Day festivities at your school.

*Tell about a special
valentine you once gave.*

_____

_____

_____

_____

_____

_____

_____

_____

February 13

*Tell about a special valentine
you once received.*

_____

_____

_____

_____

_____

_____

_____

_____

February 14

Tell about your first date.

_____

_____

_____

_____

_____

_____

_____

February 15

Tell about your first kiss.

_____

_____

_____

_____

_____

_____

February 16

*Tell about your first
favorite TV shows.*

_____

_____

_____

_____

_____

_____

February 17

Tell about family reunions
in your childhood.

What do you remember as
your favorite subject in school?

*What do your remember
as your least favorite
school subject?*

February 20

*What is the biggest
problem you remember
having in Grade School?*

February 21

*What is the biggest problem you
remember having in Jr. High school?*

February 22

*What is the biggest problem you
remember having in Sr. High school?*

February 23

*Tell about a great victory or personal
success story from your school days.*

February 24

*Did you and your friends ever
have a secret hide-out?*

February 25

*Tell about a favorite restaurant
or public place where you and
your friends liked to gather.*

February 26

*Tell about the best
pet you ever had.*

_____

_____

_____

_____

_____

_____

_____

_____

February 27

*Tell about other
pets you had.*

_____

_____

_____

_____

_____

_____

_____

_____

February 28

Tell about being in a
school play or program.

Tell about a school
principal you remember.

Did you ever pretend to be sick as an
excuse to stay home from school?

March 3

Did you ever get in trouble
for saying a bad word?

March 4

Tell about how you spent your
Saturdays during the school year.

March 5

Tell about how you
spent your Sundays.

What was the naughtiest or meanest
thing you remember doing in school?
Were there consequences?

When on car trips, did
you play car games?

Tell of a difficult essay or term paper assignment.

March 9

What radio programs or stations were your favorites?

March 10

*What was the first movie you
ever saw and who starred in it?*

_____

_____

_____

_____

_____

_____

_____

_____

_____

March 11

*What was your favorite
movie and why?*

_____

_____

_____

_____

_____

_____

_____

_____

March 12

*Did kids ever tease
you and why?*

*Do you remember
your first pizza?*

If you went to college, tell which college you chose and why.

March 15

Tell your major and how you chose it.

March 16

Tell me more about your college years, or your work experiences in early adulthood.

March 17

*What do you remember as
your favorite time of year? Why?*

March 18

*Describe some household
chores you had as a child.*

March 19

Describe some
outside chores.

March 20

Which chore did you dislike the most
and how did you try to get out of it?

Did you have a favorite chore?

March 21

What bones have you
broken and how?

March 22

Did you ever
need stitches?

March 23

Do you have any other good
stories about being injured?

March 24

Tell of a childhood illness.

March 25

Tell about an experience at the doctor's or dentist's office.

March 26

*What memories do you have of
St. Patrick's Day in your childhood?*

March 27

If you ever hitch-hiked, explain.

March 28

*Name your best
school friends.*

*Tell of a nickname given to you by
friends or classmates. How did you
get it? How did you feel about it?*

What were some crazy names
or nicknames in your school?

March 31

Do you have a good
April Fool's Day story?

April 1

Tell about a practical joke or
prank you played on someone.

April 2

Tell about a practical joke or prank someone played on you?

Did you ever make a kite? How? Tell about your kite-flying experiences.

Did you ever feel a hatred for another person? Explain.

April 5

As a child, what did you want to be when you grew up?

April 6

Did you ever bring home or
try to adopt a wild animal?

April 7

Relate a favorite
spring memory.

April 8

Did your Mom or Dad ever find
something you had hidden?

April 9

Make up a limerick about yourself.
There once was a…

Now make up a limerick about me.
There once was a…

Share a memory of going to church as you were growing up.

April 12

Share a memory about a church social activity.

April 13

Tell about an Easter Egg hunt.

April 14

Tell about any other Easter traditions.

April 15

Did you ever have a
recurring dream as a child?

April 16

When you played make-
believe, what did you pretend?

April 17

Tell about the best birthday
present you ever received.

Tell about any sports you
played in Jr. or Sr. High.

Did you ever write something
that you were really proud of?

*What was your favorite
book as a youth?*

*What is the biggest
physical problem you
had to deal with?*

*Did you have
any superstitions?*

April 23

*Where were your best
hide-and-seek places?*

April 24

*Tell about the first time you were
ever behind the wheel of a car.*

April 25

Did you ever take anything
that wasn't yours?

April 26

What did you do with it?
Did you get caught?

April 27

Do you have a story
about a big surprise?

April 28

What childhood fear
do you remember?

April 29

How much do you remember
paying for an ice cream cone?

Tell about a
May Day tradition.

What were May Baskets made of
and what did they contain?

*Did you have
a treehouse?*

*Were you ever
bitten by a dog?*

Did your mother ever
make a special gift for you?

May 5

Tell a favorite memory
of your mother.

May 6

Tell about some good advice
your mother gave you.

Relate your family Mother's Day traditions, or tell me
more about what kind of person your mother was.

Do you remember any
childhood songs or rhymes?

May 9

Name some popular hit
songs from your youth.

May 10

What was your favorite
singing group or band?

_____

_____

_____

_____

Tell a favorite singer and
a song that he/she sang?

_____

_____

_____

What kind of dances did
you do as a youth?

_____

_____

_____

Tell about the first
dance you ever went to.

Tell about your high school
prom or formal dance.

*Describe your military experience
or that of someone in your family.*

May 16

*Share a memory involving a war
during your childhood or youth.*

May 17

Share another memory involving
a war during childhood or youth.

May 18

If you have another photograph of
your childhood to share, place it here.

May 19

Tell about your graduation
exercises or traditions.

May 20

What year did you graduate from high school?
What do you recall about your feelings, emotions,
hopes and dreams at this time of your life?

May 21

How many students were in your high
school? In your graduating class?

May 22

*Did you have homework
during your school years?*

*Tell of someone you
envied and why.*

*Describe a very proud
moment in your childhood.*

_____

_____

_____

_____

_____

_____

_____

_____

May 25

*Tell about Memorial Day
traditions during your youth.*

_____

_____

_____

_____

_____

_____

_____

_____

May 26

Share a special memory
of Memorial Day.

May 27

Did you play a
musical instrument?

May 28

Tell about the closest friend
you had during your childhood.

May 29

*Is there anything you have now that
you have kept from your childhood?*

May 30

*Do you have any good
bathtime stories?*

May 31

*Tell about a strange person
that lived in your town.* ....

....

....

....

....

....

....

....

....

June 1

*Describe a place you
liked to go to be alone.* ....

....

....

....

....

....

....

....

....

June 2

*Did you ever sleep
under the stars?*

June 3

*Tell about hot dog or
marshmallow roasting.*

June 4

Did you ever go on a
camp out? Tell about it.

June 5

Did you ever go
on a snipe hunt?

June 6

Do you remember a favorite snack that you liked to make?

June 7

Share a horse-riding story.

June 8

What was your first job? How much did you get paid?

June 9

*Tell about other paying
jobs you had as a youth.*

June 10

What was your first purchase
using your own money?

June 11

If you were ever in
a parade, tell about it.

June 12

Tell another memory
about a parade.

June 13

Share a childhood memory
about a death that affected you.

June 14

Relate your happiest
memory as a youth.

June 15

How did you learn to swim?

June 16

Where did you go to swim and
what kind of suits did you wear?

June 17

Tell a favorite memory
of your father.

_____

_____

_____

_____

_____

_____

_____

_____

_____

June 18

Tell about some good
advice your father gave you.

_____

_____

_____

_____

_____

_____

_____

_____

_____

June 19

*Relate your family Father's Day
traditions, or tell me more about what
kind of person your father was.*

June 20

*Did your father ever make
a special gift for you?*

June 21

Did you have a special nature place where you went to explore?

_____

_____

_____

_____

_____

_____

_____

_____

_____

_____

_____

June 22

Did you ever go skinny-dipping?

_____

_____

_____

_____

_____

_____

_____

_____

_____

_____

June 23

*Did you ever
make mud pies?*

June 24

*Did you go barefoot in the
summer? If so, relate an experience
about stepping on something.*

June 25

*Describe a few of the favorite
hair styles of your youth.*

_____

_____

_____

_____

_____

_____

June 26

Tell about a bike you had.

_____

_____

_____

_____

_____

June 27

*Tell about your
first very own car.*

_____

_____

_____

_____

_____

June 28

*Did you ever have
or make a swing?*

June 29

*Tell about seeing something you
thought was very beautiful.*

June 30

*Describe an outside
game you made up.*

July 1

Describe an inside
game you made up.

July 2

What kind of fireworks did people
have when you were a youth?

July 3

*Tell about Independence Day
traditions of your childhood.*

July 4

*Do you have a special July 4th
that you remember most?*

July 5

Did you ever go to carnivals or amusement parks? Where?

....
....
....
....
....

July 6

What kinds of rides and games were there? How much did they cost?

....
....
....
....

July 7

Tell about any State Fair or County Fair experiences.

....
....
....
....

July 8

Tell about going to a circus, a Chautauqua, or a hometown celebration/festival.

July 9

Tell any favorite summertime memory.

July 10

*Did you go fishing, hunting
or trapping in your youth?*

July 11

*Tell about your
biggest or best catch.*

July 12

Do you remember having a favorite candy? How much did it cost?

_____

_____

_____

_____

_____

_____

_____

July 13

Tell about the first meal you ever made by yourself.

_____

_____

_____

_____

_____

July 14

Share a memory about going on a picnic.

_____

_____

_____

_____

_____

_____

July 15

What kinds of party games or
party activities were popular?

July 16

Share a memory involving
a heatwave or drought.

July 17

What did you
do to stay cool?

July 18

What was your favorite
holiday of the year? Why?

July 19

*Share a birthday
party memory.*

July 20

*Tell about the neatest shoes
you ever owned as a youth.*

July 21

*Share a memory
about a power outage.*

_____

_____

_____

_____

_____

_____

_____

July 22

*Relate a memory involving
a flood or cloudburst.*

_____

_____

_____

_____

_____

July 23

*Relate a memory of a tornado,
hurricane, or destructive wind.*

_____

_____

_____

_____

_____

July 24

*What memories do you
have of lightning or thunder
during your childhood?*

July 25

*Share a special memory
about riding in a boat.*

July 26

*Tell about a family
vacation trip.*

July 27

*Share the best vacation
experience you can recall.*

July 28

Share the most unpleasant
vacation experience you can recall.

July 29

Do you have any other
memories about a river,
lake, or beach to share?

July 30

Tell a memory about riding
on a ferry, bus, train, or plane.

July 31

If you were to return to your youth,
what would you do differently?

Describe your childhood
 home & neighborhood.

Tell about going to
a summer camp.

Tell of an experience climbing
a mountain or big hill.

Tell a memory about having company
at your house, or of a family party.

Tell about board games and card
games you played as a youth.

Did your mom or dad have a favorite remedy for when you were sick or hurt?

August 7

Share an experience about poison ivy or poison weed, a bee sting or bug bite.

August 8

What was your best talent?

August 9

Tell about a time
when you got lost.

August 10

Did you ever play in
the sprinkler or hose?

August 11

What was the dumbest stunt ever
pulled by you and a brother or sister? ....
....
....

Were there consequences? ....
....
....
....
....

August 12

Did you have any favorite family
songs that you sang together? ....
....
....
....
....
....
....

August 13

Tell about your bedroom.

_____

_____

_____

_____

_____

August 14

*Share a memory of staying
overnight with a friend.* _____

_____

_____

_____

_____

August 15

*If you ever ran away
from home, tell about it.* _____

_____

_____

_____

_____

August 16

Do you remember being really
curious about something?

Share your childhood
experiences with roller skates.

Did you ever experience home sickness?

....
....
....
....
....
....
....
....

August 19

Did you ever make a purchase that you later regretted?

....
....
....
....
....
....
....
....

August 20

*Share an early experience
with shaving.*

August 21

*Tell about a favorite doll,
teddy bear, or other stuffed toy.*

August 22

*What other toys did
you like to play with?*

August 23

*Did you have to abide by
a curfew as a youth?*

August 24

*If you ever had a hero,
tell who. Tell why.*

August 25

*Phones have changed over the
years. Describe how you used a
phone to call up a childhood friend.*

*Did you ever have a fire in your home or
accidentally catch something on fire?*

Tell about going to box socials or pot lucks.

August 28

Tell about an incident when you were very angry with your mom or dad.

August 29

*Tell about an incident when your
mom or dad was very angry with you.*

August 30

*Share a memory
involving an outhouse.*

August 31

*Do you remember any Labor
Day traditions of your youth?*

September 1

VJ Day...Do you have a memory involving
the end of World War II?
If not, then share a memory of Vietnam.

September 2

Back-To-School-Days…
What do you remember about that
big yearly "First Day of School"?

September 3

Tell about your school
year calendar.

September 4

Tell about a school bully.

September 5

What do you remember
doing at recess?

September 6

Tell about the playground
equipment at your grade school.

September 7

Did your parents ever make you
wear something stupid to school?

September 8

Tell about who you thought was
the smartest kid in school and why.

September 9

Tell about the naughtiest
kid in school.

September 10

*How did you
experience the 9/11 attacks?*

September 11

September 12

*Name the schools
that you went to.*

*What was your most
embarrassing school moment?*

*What teacher did you
dislike the most? Why?*

Describe a typical school
day outfit in grade school...

In high school...

Where did you usually
buy your clothes?

September 16

If you were ever in
a fight, tell about it.

September 17

Did you ever have a
crush on a teacher?

September 18

Who was the best teacher
you ever had? Why?

September 19

What did your report cards
usually have to say about you?

September 20

*What is the worst trick that
you remember a student
playing on a teacher?*

September 21

*What is the meanest thing that you
remember a teacher doing to a student!*

September 22

How did you get to
and from school?

Do you remember a special
school custodian?

What were your school colors?

What was your
school mascot?

September 26

Tell about a memorable
birthday cake.

September 27

Did you ever have a "good friend"
who did something mean to you?

September 28

How did your school
observe Homecoming?

September 29

Do you have any special Homecoming experiences to relate?

September 30

Did your High School have cheerleaders? What did they wear?

October 1

Can you recite any of your school cheers?

October 2

Tell about any other
extra-curricular activities.

October 3

Do you have a memory of
going to a big concert?

October 4

Do you have any special memories about raking and burning leaves, or mowing the lawn?

October 5

If you ever played in the leaves, tell about it.

October 6

Do you have some
good advice for me?

October 7

October 8

*What was your most prized
possession as a child?*

October 9

*Share a memory about
a bat in the house.*

October 10

*Relate a story about a
mouse in the house.*

October 11

What allowance did you get at
different ages during your youth?

October 12

Did you have to do
anything to earn it?

October 13

Do you have any advice on how
to be wise with my money?

October 14

What is the strangest thing
you ever saw in the sky?

October 15

*Tell about pulling
or losing a baby tooth.*

October 16

*Did you ever lose something
really important to you?*

October 17

Did you ever lose or break something that belonged to someone else?

October 18

Was an injustice ever done to you?

October 19

*Share a favorite
fall memory.*

October 20

*Do you have a story about
standing up against odds for
something you really believed in?*

October 21

*What is the farthest you
ever ran or walked?*

October 22

Did you ever pick apples?

If you had a watch,
tell about it.

*What hobbies or collections
did you have as a youth?*

October 25

*Share a memory about
being very scared.*

October 26

Tell a story about a time when
you dressed up in a costume.

October 27

Did you ever tell ghost stories?

October 28

Do you have a good ghost or haunted house story to relate?

_____
_____
_____
_____
_____
_____

October 29

What did people do at Halloween?

_____
_____
_____
_____
_____

October 30

Do you have a special Halloween memory?

_____
_____
_____
_____
_____

October 31

November questions will deal with your courtship, marriage,
and my arrival in the world.

Tell about how you first knew my mother.

November 1

Tell about your first date with her.

November 2

What qualities first attracted you to her?

November 3

Tell about how you proposed marriage to my mom.

_____

_____

_____

_____

_____

_____

_____

If you have a picture taken during your courtship to share, place it here.

_____

_____

_____

_____

_____

_____

When and where
were you married?

What did you wear?

Who performed the ceremony?
Who stood up with you?

November 8

Tell about any other circumstances
of your wedding day.

November 9

Did you go on a honeymoon?

November 10

Veteran's Day…
Name the veterans in your family
and times during which they served.

November 11

*Tell about where you
lived when first married.*

November 12

*What was your
job at the time?*

November 13

*What qualities in my mom did
you try unsuccessfully to change?*

November 14

Tell about the most serious problem or challenge you faced during your early years of marriage.

November 15

Tell the full names, birthdays, and birthplaces of all of your children.

November 16

Tell about the
day I was born.

November 17

How did you
choose my name?

November 18

What other names did
you consider for me?

Many people remember just
what they were doing when they
heard of the assassination of
John F. Kennedy. If you are not
old enough to have that time
etched in your memory, relate
any other childhood story.

*Who was the President
when I was born?*

November 21

*If you have a baby picture of
me to share, place it here.*

November 22

*What was the address of
my first childhood home?*

November 23

What do you remember most
about my first month of life?

November 24

What were my other
childhood addresses?

November 25

*Share your favorite funny
story of me as a child.*

November 26

*Share a favorite
Thanksgiving memory.*

November 27

Tell about the Thanksgiving traditions of your youth. What foods were on your Thanksgiving table?

November 28

Tell your all-time favorites:

Food-

Book-

Movie-

November 29

More favorites:

TV Show-

Song-

Color-

November 30

More favorites:

    Bible verse- ....

....

....

....

    Pastime- ....

....

....

....

....

December 1

As a youth, who was your favorite movie star? Why? ....

....

....

....

....

....

....

....

December 2

Use the next 3 entries for anything else you would like me to know about your childhood.

December 3

December 4

December 5

Do you have any
knowledge of how your
first name was chosen?

December 6

Pearl Harbor Day…
If you are not old enough to relate
a memory of that day, relate any
other childhood remembrance.

December 7

Tell about something you built,
designed, or made as a youth.

December 8

Tell about your favorite
stores to browse in as a child.

December 9

What did you like
to look at there?

December 10

Were you ever in a church or school
Christmas or Holiday pageant?

December 11

When did you put up your Christmas tree?
Where did you get them? ....

....

....

....

December 12

How did you decorate your trees? ....

....

....

....

....

December 13

Did you hang a Christmas stocking? ....

....

....

....

....

December 14

Did your Grandpa or Grandma ever make gifts for you? Tell about them.

December 15

Tell about the neatest present you remember giving to your mom.

December 16

Tell about the neatest present you remember giving to your dad.

December 17

Tell about the best Christmas present you ever received, as a child.

December 18

*Tell about the worst Christmas present
you ever received, as a child.*

December 19

*Tell about your experiences
with Santa Claus.*

December 20

*Do you remember a "best"
Christmas of childhood?*

December 21

*Tell about Holiday
celebrations at a relative's
house during your childhood.*

December 22

*Did your family observe
the birth of Jesus at
Christmas? In what ways?*

December 23

*Tell about the most memorable
gifts you have given me.*

December 24

Tell about the most memorable
gifts I have given you.

December 25

Share any other
Christmas memory.

December 26

Is there anything else that you would like me to know about __my__ childhood?

December 27

December 28

*Do you remember celebrating
any special wedding anniversaries
of your parents or grandparents?*

December 29

*What special memories
do you have of New Year's
Eve or New Year's Day?*

December 30

*If you were to make a
New Year's Resolution this
year, what might it be?*

December 31

Memory Journals for Special People

Grandma, Tell Me Your Memories – Heirloom Edition

Grandpa, Tell Me Your Memories – Heirloom Edition

Mom, Share Your Life With Me – Heirloom Edition

Dad, Share Your Life With Me – Heirloom Edition

Grandma, Tell Me Your Memories

Grandpa, Tell Me Your Memories

Mom, Share Your Life With Me

Dad, Share Your Life With Me

To the Best of My Recollection

To My Dear Friend

My Days...My Pictures

My Days...My Writings

My Life...My Thoughts

Sisters

Mom, Tell Me One More Story...Your Story of Raising Me

Dad, Tell Me One More Story...Your Story of Raising Me